Whispers Of The Soul

Poems Celebrating Love, Resilience, and Human Experience

MINISHA H. PEREIRA

Made with ❤ on the BookLeaf Publishing Platform
www.bookleafpub.in
www.bookleafpub.com

Dedication

This book is dedicated to my friends, loved ones, and all who have enriched my journey. Your presence has illuminated my path, allowing me to experience life in its most beautiful form. For your love, support, and the moments we've shared, I am forever grateful.

Preface

"Whispers of the Soul" is a captivating poetry collection that beautifully captures the essence of the human experience. Weaving together themes of love, spirituality, personal growth, and social consciousness, the author invites readers on a heartfelt journey of introspection. Through each verse, the collection explores the experiences that shape our lives, reminding us of the beauty found in connection, gratitude, and the power of love.

Whether shared as a gift or treasured by the reader, this collection offers a meaningful way to express gratitude and strengthen the bonds with those we hold dear. It serves as a timeless reminder of the importance of love and the profound strength we gain from the relationships we nurture.

The Collection Highlights

Spiritual Foundations

- *No Greater Love*
- *Beyond the Beads*
- *Unworthy Yet Loved*
- *Love's Ocean*
- *Grateful Heart*

Family and Personal Tribute

- *My Guiding Light*
- *Mother's Love*
- *Twin flame*
- *Divine Friendship*
- *Devotion and Bonds*

Reflections on Life's Journey

- *Bittersweet Journey of Dreaming*
- *Life's Cricket Match*
- *Navigating Life's Journey*
- *Expectations Clash*
- *Power of Smile*

Celebrating Universal Beauty and Justice

- *Pledge to Mother Nature*
- *Call for Equality*
- *Essence of Companionship*
- *Mystical Gaze*
- *Essence of Friendship*
- *Rainbow Cake Reflection*

Acknowledgements

*__Every good and perfect gift is from above,__
__coming down from the Father of lights, with__
__whom there is no variation or shadow of__
__turning__"* – **James 1:17.**
I thank the Lord for blessing me with the grace
to understand, to love, and, most importantly, to
be grateful for all that I have. Everything I am
and everything I have, I owe to Him.

1. No Greater Love

Loving without condition is a gift from above,
To share real affection with a heart full of love.
Can we humans, love each other this way,
Selflessly giving ourselves without expecting a say?
Our love often falls short, bound and confined,
Its depths reach far less than our hearts and minds.

True love is elusive, a question unending,
A feeling that grows beyond only pretending.
In this world of self-interest, can human love endure?
To answer, let me share a story of love steadfast and
pure.

Long ago, a humble King was born on Earth,
A life lived in simplicity, a gift beyond worth.
He saw no caste, no creed, no shade,
Only love in each sacrifice he made.
Through scorn and abuse, without raising a hand,
He faced every trial in a harsh, hostile land.

For us, He endured, so we might truly live;
Through all His suffering, only love did He give.
With thorns for a crown and nails piercing skin,
bearing all our darkness, forgiving our sins.
Giving His life, with no debt of His own,
for the love of our Father might be fully known.
Every drop of blood shed, not for His wrong,
But for sins that are ours, deep and long.
What love can compare, selfless and grand?
Jesus gave all; a love none can withstand.

No greater love could this world ever see
Than the love that Christ gave for you and me.

2. Beyond the Beads

Praying the Rosary holds a place of high worth,
A sacred practice, our refuge on earth.
It helps us triumph over the darkest night,
Guiding us toward peace, bringing us light.

With life-giving grace, cherished and known,
Meditating on sacred mysteries where truth is shown.
But is the Rosary prayed with true intention?
Or spoken out loud without reflection.

In today's world, social media has taken the pace,
Its few rewards are shadowed by much we misplace.
We time our prayers to fit our routines,
Yet the Rosary's power remains unseen.

Some claim that praying takes too much time,
Unaware it's our world that remains blind.
Pray the Rosary if you love Mama Mary;
Her joy lies in this gift we humbly carry.

Few perceive the blessings this mystery brings,
The peace and wisdom that heal life's stings.
I testify, friends: give a few moments or an hour,
And encounter God's Grace, His blessings, and His
power.
turning our hearts toward true transformation,
Embracing new insight and renewed dedication.
To walk by His words, to forgive and to love,
And find our place in His kingdom above.

3. Unworthy Yet Loved

Jesus, You see me when I'm fallen away,
You wipe my tears and show me the way.
You know the worst and best for my soul,
You guide my steps, though I may not know.

You never impose but gently lead,
Accepting me as I am, in every need.
Though I falter, though I stray,
You watch over me every day.

Even when I fail, when I'm not whole,
You cleanse me with Your blood and make me bold.
You wash away the stain of my sin
And leave me renewed from within.

With all my flaws, my heart still cries,
"I am Yours, though I'm not wise."
But You whisper gently, "My child, you are loved,
Just as you are, by the grace from above."

How grateful I am for Your endless grace,
There is none like You, Lord! No sweeter embrace.
I love You, Jesus, for taking me in,
Though unworthy, You call me Your own again.

4. Love's Ocean

Love is a precious gift from above,
Its essence is so rare, moving us with love.
Love seeks deeply, it always gives,
Never quick to judge, but quick to forgive.
Love is the greatest treasure, fulfilling every heart's
desire,
It ignites passion within us, setting our souls on fire.

How sorrowful are those who cannot see,
The vastness of love gentle decree.
I pray that God blesses them with hearts as pure as a
dove,
So they may experience the awe of Divine love

How can one tell when love is truly divine?
It's a bond that joins two souls in a cosmic rhyme.
Blessed are those who dive in love endless sea,
For their love will rise above all adversity.
Two souls united, devoted to grace,
Embracing God's guidance in a spiritual embrace.

5. Grateful Heart

Everything we are, all we hold, is a blessing from above,
But do we thank Him or take for granted His endless
love?
We question His presence in times of strife,
Yet He gave His Son to provide us with life."

How wonderful is the one, who loves us unconditionally,
Not that we deserve but He loves us infinitely.
Let us pause to reflect and give thanks,
For His kindness and the blessings we bank.

Thank Him for rescuing us from our plight,
His unwavering love guides us every night.

6. My Guiding Light

When life grew tangled and shadows swayed,
Strength was the power he needed each day.
With virtues as guides, he shaped his fate,
Overcoming disasters that others would hate.

He wasn't born with the finest or best,
But his spirit always set him apart from the rest.
Never alone, and never gave in,
That's why he was blessed with a throne to win!

Too many challenges stood in his way,
But he rose above them, come what may.
Living with joy and cherishing life,
Ignoring the world's noise, valuing what's right.
Through each barrier, he stayed on track,
Never turning, never looking back.

As each year passes, I honor this wonderful soul,
Whose calmness softens our family as a whole.
A maestro in spirit, inspiring me,

Guiding my steps timely.
Without him, my life's story would stall,
A page unturned, a path too small.

Thank you, God, for My precious gem,
Who lifted me when my light grew dim.
When life was tough, he stayed near,
His eyes saw victory beyond my fear.
His faith was the force that helped me through,
A light so steady, a love so true.

Thank you, Dad, for making me strong,
For a love to which I've always belonged.
To God, I pray, with all of my heart,
To bless you with treasures that never part.
This is the one prayer I humbly say,
To bless my father, every single day.

7. Mother's Love

Among God's wonders and all His creations,
The finest gift is our mother's dedication.
So gentle, yet fierce in her loving embrace,
With strength to protect, no challenge is too great.

I am honored to thank God above,
For my mom, she fills our lives with love.
How often do we forget the sacrifices they've made,
The sleepless nights they endured when we were in pain.
Mothers have gifts that make them wise,
From their soothing meals to their caring advice.

Each day, they work to keep smiles on our faces,
Finding joy in us, not in life's race.
How blessed we are with such a rare treasure,
But do we thank them without measure?
Too often, we overlook their worth,
Failing to appreciate their hard work.

Sometimes, in a world of selfish routines,

In their old age, we send them away to places unseen.
as God's children, loving and kind,
Keep our mothers close, with peace of mind.
Mothers are angels, sent from above;
Let's honor them fully, with reverence and love.
For in caring for them, we honor the Divine,
Far more than any distant shrine.

8. Twin Flame

A companion whose kindness and care are always clear,
A constant support as life's challenges appear
In times of need, a calm soul to repair,
Their presence brings energy beyond compare.

How blessed is one touched by such grace,
A radiant soul whose charm lights up the place.
Though sometimes communication falters of pride,
A divine bond holds, deep and wide.

Two souls united in love's tender embrace,
In compassion, truth, and a spiritual space.
Sharing a love that words can't define,
A bond that transcends place and time.
What is it that empowers these souls so whole?
A love that completes, two hearts and one goal.

Can such love be explained or named?
It's a Divine Twin Flame, a mystery untamed.

9. Divine Friendship

True friends are rare, hard to find,
They captivate your heart, soul, and mind.
meeting them first as strangers, unaware,
Not knowing when they'll truly care.

True friends will give their lives for you,
Their love and loyalty are forever true.
But why do they share such devotion and grace?
Because their affection knows no boundary, no space.

True friends do more than dry your tears,
They've been carrying your pain through the years.
Do we create such friendships, the ones we long for?
Or, when they come, do we falter and ignore?

My dear friends, open your eyes to see,
If such a soul is walking with thee.
They'll not only help you grow and rise,
But also heal thee, in ways beyond the skies.
If you find a friend like this, so rare,

Hold them close, treat them with care.

For they are a blessing, beyond what's known,
A divine friendship, pure and overthrown.

10. Devotion and Bonds

How can I convey my devotion to you?
As pure and refreshing as the morning dew.
Along my journey, I've met many souls,
Each one is a treasure, beyond what words can hold.

We share not just joys, but sorrows too,
Together, we bless each other with hope anew.
It is my delight, and that's why I'll declare,
Friends like you are rare beyond compare!

At times, I pause and reflect on our bond,
The depth of our friendship is truly profound.
A motherly love that nurtures and cares,
Offering wisdom in moments of despair.

Gentle reminders when mistakes come to light,
You help steer the way, making things right.
A companion who shares both the good and bad,
Every meal, every shopping spree we've had.

Through joy, sorrow, and even rage,
Our spirits are entwined on life's vibrant stage.
Without these moments, friendship grows still,
But together, we flourish, our hearts always will!

11. Bittersweet Journey of Dreaming

The act of dreaming can bring such delight,
If you believe in your strength to face every plight.
The joy in dreaming is a treasure worth holding,
Their triumphs unfold like a story unfolding.

what if your hopes shatter in an instant,
Like a mine once filled, now hollow and distant?
It may sting for a while, yet soon you'll find,
the heart that bears wounds, with scars of every kind.

So ponder your visions before they take flight,
For they hold the power of joy and fright.
In dreams lies a duality, a bittersweet chance,
To taste both the thrill and the ache of the dance.

12. Life's Cricket Match

Life's a cricket match where you play your role,
Swinging for fences, aiming for your goal.
Though we strive to sidestep each challenge, each day,
When desires meet hardship, that's when we pray.

With obstacles all around us, we often feel troubled,
What choices are left in a world so muddled?
Yet souls may differ in their response to the game;
In the face of frustration, no path is the same.

Life's course can shift with the player's intent;
Success lies hidden in how time is spent.
The world transforms through the lens we hold,
For a striver or dreamer, new stories unfold.

The real winner isn't the one who seems bold,
But one who builds greatness from nothing at all.
Daily challenges arise, but they're lessons profound,
Each one has a chance to stay firm and stand your
ground.

So, embrace the game, with its highs and lows;
Each setback is a chance to let resilience show.
Life is a journey, a match we all play,
And in the end, it's growth that lights the way.

13. Navigating Life's Journey

Everything can change in life, and oh, so fast,
Yet we can hold on tight, to what shouldn't slip past.
Blessed is the soul who foresees tomorrow,
Navigating with grace through waves of sorrow.

Obstacles arise as we journey along,
And when we're tempted to stray, it feels so wrong.
But in that moment of discerning right from wrong,
We must stand our ground and be steadfastly strong.

One must be bold, not only for their fight,
But for those who seek to share in their victorious light.
Leave tears behind, step toward with grace,
embracing a smile that uplifts every heart in place.

The truest path to joy, a life well led,
Is to release the past and let go of dread.
In shedding our burdens, stress, and fear clear,
And under the Divine's touch, blessings will appear.

14. Expectations Clash

Expectations from loved ones are natural,
Yet absent in bonds that feel more formal.
High hopes often show the depth of affection,
For those we adore, with no need for correction.

But what if your hopes stretch beyond their bounds?
That's a danger, my friends, where trouble resounds.
When desires go unmet, it weighs heavy and deep,
Causing trust to waver, making hearts weep.

How hard it can be to accept such a fate,
Recognizing its power to suffocate.
In that moment, find the right course,
With resolve, you can restore the source.

A true love knows no limits or walls,
So why let expectations cause it to fall?

15. Power of Smile

I relish sinking, for each time I rise,
I grow Wiser, with new insight.
I long to smile, even while I'm crying,
For life's lessons teach us to keep trying.

A jewel magnificent, concealing our pain,
A smile brightens the days like sunshine after rain.
Who is truly blessed to find joy through despair?
They show their faith in God, trusting His care.

Blessed is the soul who lets go of strife,
Grateful to God for each breath in life.
A smile is the simplest gift we can share,
So why not offer it freely, spreading joy everywhere?

16. Pledge to Mother Nature

As I lay in my comfy bed, a thought fills my mind,
Do we take pride in our achievements yet still be so
blind?
In this modern world, are we egocentric and vain?
Supposedly mighty, yet we cause Nature such pain.

Nature, sculpted by God's hand, a beauty so pure,
Created with love, as the holy scriptures assure.
How can we destroy such a Divine creation?
We lack the authority for such devastation.

To observe and protect Nature's wonders is our call,
To cherish its worth and prevent its downfall.
Admiring and preserving is our noble quest,
Recognizing her beauty, we must do our best.

So let us dive into an ocean of love and light,
Vowing to protect what sustains our life's might.

17. Call for Equality

God granted us privileges by forming us unique,
Creating in His image, with the power to speak.
Not to forget his everlasting blessings on us all?
Yet we often stand by injustices that take their toll.

Let us reflect: Do we truly uphold equality's way,
Or drift with the tide, letting fairness decay?
Gender, caste, and faith still divide our land,
At times, gender inequality takes root, and stretches its
hand.
Men are seen as the providers, the ones who lead,
While women are dismissed, bound by roles decreed.

And what of our transgender siblings, mocked with cruel
jest,
Their pain was ignored, their dignity suppressed.
When I confront these issues, one thought fills my mind:
I long for a nation where compassion's blind.

In every field, business, science, or politics,

May women rise, their brilliance no longer fixed.
leadership all praised, especially in the COVID fight,
Proving their strength, their power, their light.

So why can't we respect women in society?
A woman in different roles is a gift to humanity.
It pains me deeply to witness rapes and murders unfold,
Committed to filthy pleasures, turning pure hearts cold.

How can we discuss equality when our actions betray
our kind?
Are we ashamed of the cruelty that darkens our minds?
We visit holy places, seeking blessings from the divine,
Yet fail to act, fighting against Mother Nature's design.
Even Nature cares for us abundantly, without
discrimination,
So let us strive to make equality a reality in our nation.

18. Essence of Companionship

Companionship isn't measured by time,
It's a bond that grows, through joy or grime.
Strong through the good, resilient in the bad,
Even in clashes, when emotions make us mad.

A true companion may take time to find,
But can bloom in a glance or smile, unconfined.
A true mate may not always touch your soul,
But through shared moments, they make you whole.

Grateful to those who've brightened my way,
Easing my strife and making each day.
I apologize if my words caused you pain,
No ill intent, just a playful refrain.

Thank you for your cheer, grace, and support,
Your kindness is always a heartfelt escort.
To all my friends, loved or not,
Love is abundant, and hearts that truly count.

19. Mystical Gaze

It's all about those eyes, so deep, so rare,
Their passionate gaze holds me captive; it's only fair
To linger, not turn away, from their silent lore,
Innocent as a child, yet wise like those who've seen
more.

These eyes are a portal, drawing me in,
To glimpse your soul, where the stars begin.
How can one not be enchanted, lost in their gaze,
Eyes that speak love in a thousand ways?

It's not my fault, this magic I feel,
I thank the heavens above for making it real.

20. Essence of Friendship

How can I convey my devotion to you,
As pure and fresh as the morning dew?
I've met so many friends along my way,
Each one is a treasure, more than words can say.

Not only do they share our joys and sorrows,
But together, we bring hope for tomorrow.
It's my delight, and that's why I want to share,
Friends like mine are so rare, so fair!

At times, I pause and reflect on the bond,
For the nature of our friendship is far beyond.
A motherly love that nurtures, that cares,
Offering wisdom in moments that ensnare.

With gentle reminders when mistakes are clear,
They guide my path, making everything dear.
A companion who shares both good and bad,
In every shared meal, in every spree, we've had.

Through joy and sorrow, and even through rage,
Our spirits unite on life's vibrant stage.
Without these moments, friendship would still,
But together we flourish, our hearts always will.

21. Rainbow Cake Reflection

As I savored a rainbow cake,
Iced with frost, topped with white chocolate,
It seemed drab outside, unremarkable to see,
But one slice revealed colors, vibrant and free!

At times, our lives may seem dull and plain,
Like the crust of a cake, simple, mundane.
But true beauty emerges at the core,
When we take the time to explore and seek more.

When one dares to delve deep, the soul shines bright,
A journey of self-discovery, a quest for light.
So, never stray from the goals you hold dear,
For they shape a soul that's strong and clear.

A soul ready to serve, with compassion and grace,
For the betterment of mankind, and nature's embrace.

* 9 7 8 9 3 6 9 5 4 7 3 1 9 *